"To Baby Harvey, who is gaining weight quickly, and to
babies everywhere — once seen, never forgotten."
— M.M.

"To my mom and my little girl, Ava."
— A.C.

Library of Congress Control Number: 2020945077

Published by Creston Books, LLC
Berkeley, California
www.crestonbooks.co

ISBN 978-1-939547-66-8

Printed and bound in China
5 4 3 2 1

BOARDWALK BABIES

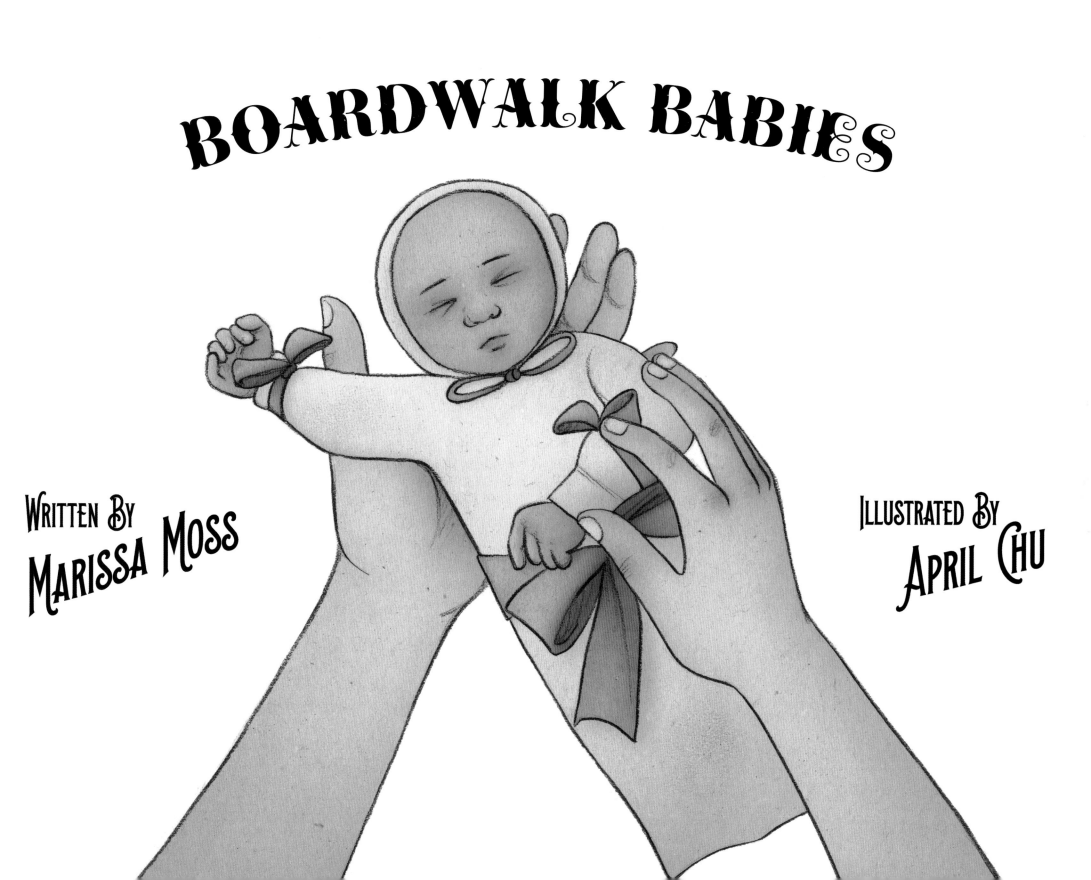

WRITTEN BY
MARISSA MOSS

ILLUSTRATED BY
APRIL CHU

"Step right up and see the tiny babies! Babies so small, you could hold them in one hand! Don't pass the babies by!"

Crowds followed the carnival barker to where he pointed, beyond Lionel the Lion-faced Man, Francis the Four-legged Woman, and the Sword Swallowers.

Inside the brick building, the room didn't look like a side show at all. Nurses in crisp white uniforms took care of the tiniest babies imaginable, kept warm and snug in glass boxes hung from the walls.

But it didn't sound like a hospital, not quiet and hushed.

"Ooooh!" a woman squealed. "That baby's head is the size of a plum!"

"This one is absolutely adorable!" another one cooed. "Such a tiny face!"

A man and a woman gazed into another incubator. "She's getting bigger," the woman said to the man.

He nodded. "She'll come home soon."

A tall man in overalls ambled in, carrying a hat box. He looked like a farmer searching for the livestock exhibits. But he strode right over to another man wearing a white doctor's coat.

"You're Dr. Couney? My wife just had our baby and he's so small, the doc said we should give up on him, but we can't. We just can't."

"Of course not!" Dr. Couney said. "Bring your son here and we'll take good care of him."

The man opened up the hat box. "Here he is, Doc."

If Dr. Couney was surprised that the box was a baby carrier, he didn't show it. He smiled and reached in for the teeny baby, wrapped in a towel. "Nurse Recht over there will take your information. I'll take care of your son."

Boardwalk babies? Incubator side shows? What was Dr. Couney thinking?

He was thinking of saving lives.

In the late 19th century, hospitals considered premature babies doomed to die. They had no idea how to care for them, so they didn't. Then Dr. Budin in Paris noticed the heat lamp that kept chicks warm. That gave him the idea to develop an incubator. It was a radical idea, one hospitals didn't trust. Dr. Budin needed a way to sell the medical world on caring for these tiny babies instead of giving up on them.

The Berlin Exposition of 1896 could be his chance. The show organizers were calling for exhibitors, especially those in science and mechanics. Dr. Budin sent a young doctor who was studying with him to set up an exhibit of incubators, a demonstration of how the warming boxes could save these babies. That young doctor was Martin Couney.

Martin set up the six incubators in the exhibit hall, but even with all the charts and diagrams he'd made, the empty boxes didn't seem like miracle machines. How could he change people's minds this way?

Martin knew what he needed — babies, actual premature babies. He could give them the chance they needed to survive while proving how well the incubators worked. Now he just needed to find some babies who needed his help.

Berlin's Charity Hospital was a big, stern-looking building. The person in charge was the Empress Augusta Victoria herself, also big and stern-looking. "What is it you want?" she barked at Dr. Couney.

Martin brought out letters testifying to his skill as a doctor, he showed her the designs for the incubator, he explained how this new invention could save the tiniest of newborns.

"You want some premature babies? To exhibit to the public?"

"I'm not exhibiting the babies, your Majesty, but the miracle machines. It's important that the medical community understands what a difference an incubator can make."

He expected the empress to slam down her fist. He thought she would shoo him away.

Instead, she nodded her head. "Take as many as you want. They have a better chance with you than with us."

Certificate

ALL the WORLD
LOVES A
BABY!

Martin called the exhibit The Child Hatchery. Although Dr. Budin had applied for the scientific section, the incubators were placed in the amusement area, sandwiched between the Congo Village and the Tyrolean Yodelers. That gave Martin an idea — he would make his exhibit the most entertaining of all. He dressed the babies in too-big clothes so they seemed even smaller. He hung up slogans on the walls along with the technical explanations.

It worked! The tiny babies were a huge success — and all survived.

Martin knew he was a good doctor, but now he discovered he was a brilliant showman. He made enough money from entry tickets to come to the United States where he hoped hospitals would be quicker to adopt incubator care. He opened the first American Baby Incubator exhibit in Buffalo, New York at the 1901 Pan-American Exposition. The babies were such a hit that one newspaper wrote that there were two must-see features of the grand 1901 show — Niagara Falls and the Baby Incubators.

The public loved seeing the tiny babies grow and thrive, but hospitals still had their doubts. Incubators seemed like silly gadgets. Martin refused to give up. If hospitals wouldn't put premature babies in incubators, then he would.

And so the Baby Incubators became a permanent part of Coney Island in 1903. Martin could care for babies there all summer while selling the public on incubator technology. When he applied for exhibit space, he checked off the "Miscellaneous" category.

The incubators weren't a ride, a show, or a food stall, but they could definitely be an attraction. The Coney Island guidebook described the exhibit as "an educational journey through a miniature hospital where premature infants first see the light of day. Boardwalk next to the steeplechase."

Martin was careful to provide the best care for the babies, as if they were in a real hospital. He hired nurses to be there around the clock and trained them to feed the newborns. One of those nurses, Annabelle May, became his wife.

All children were accepted, even the tiniest, just over one pound. It didn't matter what religion they were, the color of their skin, or how poor the parents were. Families weren't charged anything for the care their children got. Instead the entrance fees paid for everything.

Some Jewish parents tied a red string around their babies' wrists, Italians tucked in amulets warding off the evil eye. One Armenian baby arrived with a garlic necklace to give it strength. And most of them survived.

Martin loved all of the babies. He cared for them as if they were his own. And then his own daughter was born — too early and too tiny. Hildegard spent her first summer at the Coney Island sideshow. Every day Martin weighed and measured her. Every day Annabelle fed her special baby formula. And every day, Hildegard got stronger and bigger.

She was why Martin had chosen to care for these tiny babies. He hadn't known it when he started out, but he knew it now, seeing her bundled up next to the other Incubator Babies.

"I was waiting for you," he whispered to tiny Hildegard, "learning how to be the best doctor I could for you. And the best father."

Finally Hildegard was big enough to leave the incubator. But as a little girl, she came back to visit the exhibit after school. As a big girl, she started working there, cleaning up and feeding the babies.

Some of those babies came back to say thank you.

Baby Beth Allen (1 lb, 10 oz) and her parents came every Father's Day to visit with the doctor and thank him for his help. Baby Lucille (2 lbs) came back as a young woman to thank him. The Cohen triplets, Rebecca, Rosie, and Rachel (all under 2 lbs) visited as healthy, active three-year-olds after their summer in the Buffalo exhibit.

But the baby who thanked him most of all was Hildegard. "You gave me life, Poppa," she said. "And then you saved my life. And then you showed me what I was meant to do with my life. I want to save babies the way you do."

Martin, Annabelle, and Hildegard, now a nurse like her mother, worked side by side at the side show. Every year, Martin thought he would close down the exhibit, that hospitals would start housing their own incubators, but that took far longer than the doctor could ever have guessed. For nearly 40 years, Martin saved babies on the Coney Island boardwalk. Six thousand five hundred babies grew up because of him.

Hospitals finally started using incubators regularly themselves in 1943, and it was time to close the Baby Incubator exhibit.

"Once seen, never forgotten!" the barker called one last time. "All the world loves a baby!"

"I couldn't pass those babies by," said Martin softly. Annabelle took one hand. Hildegard took the other. Together, the family walked down the boardwalk one last time. Salt water taffy, the guess-your-weight man, and the tilt-a-whirl, but no more sideshow babies.

Author's Note

Martin Couney was born in Germany, but studied medicine in France under Dr. Pierre Budin, one of the early advocates of using incubators to care for premature babies. Budin used an incubator that was developed by his own mentor, Dr. Stephane Tanier, the first warm-air device created for that purpose. The French hospitals at the time considered the "peanut roaster" a gimmick and continued to use hot water bottles to try to warm the tiny babies, despite Budin's urgent pleas to change medical care for these most vulnerable newborns.

The first exhibit Dr. Couney put on, the one in Berlin in 1896, brought the novel idea of the incubator in front of a large public. People were so taken with the tiny babies, Couney was invited to exhibit all over the world, starting in London, then America, Mexico, and Brazil.

Couney was a great showman and knew how to get attention for his cause. He had one nurse slip her large diamond ring over the smallest wrists to demonstrate just how tiny these babies were. He also fed the carnival barkers their lines, telling them how best to draw in crowds. One of the early barkers at Coney Island was a charming young man named Archibald Leach, better known later as the dashing Cary Grant.

Though a talented promoter, Couney was a medical professional first and foremost. Julius H. Hess, the leading American expert on premature infants, relied on Couney's work and acknowledged him in the book he wrote on the subject in 1922. "I desire to acknowledge my indebtedness to Dr. Martin Couney for his many helpful suggestions in the preparation of the material for this book." He thanked Couney again in his later book on infant feeding. "To Dr. Martin Couney I affectionately inscribe this effort to put into practice the experiences of a quarter of a century. The thoughts on premature infants were largely stimulated by his devotion to the welfare of these small infants."

Despite caring for some of the sickest and smallest newborns, the survival rate for the Incubator Babies was extraordinary, 81%, much higher than that of preemies left in hospitals. In 1937, the New York Medical Society recognized the doctor for his exceptional work and presented him with a certificate and a watch.

Dr. Couney funded the babies' care entirely through admission fees, beginning with 10 cents a ticket when the exhibit first opened in 1903, ending at 25 cents by the time it closed in 1943. Those shiny coins paid for the incubators themselves, all the other equipment, as well as the highly-trained staff of doctors and nurses. Couney himself lived near the boardwalk so he could be close to his small patients.

A historical marker on the boardwalk in Atlantic City commemorates the Incubator Exhibit. It reads, "Dr. Couney was the first person in the United States to offer specialized care for premature infants."

Selected Bibliography

Silverman, William A. "The Incubator-Baby Side Show." *Pediatrics*, vol. 64, no. 2, 1979, pp. 127-141.

Liebling, A. J. "A Patron of the Preemies." *The New Yorker,* June 3, 1932, pp. 20-24.

"Preemie Reunion." *The New York Times*, August 1, 1904, p.7

Staff, NPR. "Babies On Display: When A Hospital Couldn't Save Them, A Sideshow Did." NPR, NPR, 10 July 2015, www.npr.org/2015/07/10/421239869/babies-on-display-when-a-hospital-couldnt-save-them-a-sideshow-did.

About the Authors

Marissa Moss is an award-winning author of more than seventy children's books. She's known for her trademark journal style, invented in the *Amelia's Notebook* series and for her many books featuring historical figures that should be known but have been forgotten by time. Her most recent is the award-winning *The Eye That Never Sleeps: How Detective Pinkerton Saved President Lincoln.*

April Chu has won awards for her gorgeous illustrations in *Ada Byron Lovelace and the Thinking Machine* and *In a Village by the Sea.* She studied architecture and infuses that knowledge of detail and perspective into her art. Her work has been featured in the Society of Illustrator's Original Art Show.

"Fascinating true story about a compassionate doctor and
showman who saved the lives of thousands of premature babies.
Beautiful sepia toned illustrations perfectlycapture the time period."
— Julie Downing, award-winning author-illustrator